The Covenant We Practice

George T. Brooks Sr.

NASHVILLE, TENNESSEE

Copyright © 2016 by Townsend Press
All rights reserved.

No part of this book may be reproduced or transmitted in any form, by any means, electronic or mechanical, including photocopying, recording, or by any information storage or retrieval system without the expressed permission in writing from the publisher. Permission requests may be addressed to Townsend Press, 330 Charlotte Avenue, Nashville, Tennessee 37201-1188; or e-mailed to customercare@sspbnbc.com.

Unless otherwise noted, Scripture quotations are from the New American Standard Bible®. Copyright © 1960, 1962, 1963, 1968, 1971, 1972, 1973, 1975, 1977, 1995 by The Lockman Foundation. Used by permission. (www.Lockman.org)

ISBN 978-1-939225-82-5
Printed in the United States of America
24 23 22 21 20 19 18 17 16 — 10 9 8 7 6 5 4 3 2 1

Contents

Introduction 5

The Church Covenant 6

Chapter 1
Salvation and Witnesses to the Covenant 7

Chapter 2
Relationship to the Church 13

Chapter 3
Relationship with the Family, the Community,
and the World 30

Chapter 4
Living Together as Christians 45

Chapter 5
Church Membership 52

About the Author 54

Introduction

The church covenant is a statement of what we believe the obligations of church members to be. The church is made up of individual church members who are equal in privileges and responsibilities. The church covenant sheds light on the privileges to be enjoyed by church members and the responsibilities to be shared.

The church covenant is an agreement that we will carry out the teachings of the Bible to the best of our ability. All of the principles of the church covenant are based upon the Word of God. As church members practice this covenant, they practice the Word of God.

The church covenant is a pledge by church members to glorify God and promote the continuation of their church. Through the practicing of this covenant, church members enhance their own spiritual growth and development. At the same time, they enhance the spiritual growth and development of the church where they hold membership.

The church covenant is not a creed (an accepted system of beliefs of a religious group). It is a declaration of what we believe the Bible to teach. In this covenant, church members have the opportunity to study some of the doctrines of the Baptist church. The reader will notice that the doctrines and beliefs of the Baptist church cover the whole Bible.

This book was written in such a way that it is only a guide into the Word of God. The writer believes that the Word of God is the only book of authority on what Christians are to believe and practice. The writer hopes that each reader of this book will follow this guide into the Word of God.

The Church Covenant

Having been led, as we believe, by the Spirit of God to receive the Lord Jesus Christ as our Savior, and on the profession of our faith, having been baptized in the name of the Father, and of the Son, and of the Holy Spirit, we do now in the presence of God, angels, and this assembly, most solemnly and joyfully enter into covenant with one another, as one body in Christ.

We engage, therefore, by the aid of the Holy Spirit, to walk together in Christian love; to strive for the advancement of this church, in knowledge, holiness, and comfort; to promote its prosperity and spirituality; to sustain its worship, ordinances, discipline, and doctrines; to contribute cheerfully and regularly to the support of the ministry, the expenses of the church, the relief of the poor, and the spread of the gospel through all nations.

We also engage to maintain family and secret devotions; to religiously educate our children; to seek the salvation of our kindred and acquaintances; to walk circumspectly in the world; to be just in our dealings, faithful in our engagements, and exemplary in our deportment; to avoid all tattling, backbiting, and excessive anger; to abstain from the sale of, and use of, intoxicating drinks as a beverage; and to be zealous in our efforts to advance the kingdom of our Savior.

We further engage to watch over one another in brotherly love; to remember one another in prayer; to aid one another in sickness and distress; to cultivate Christian sympathy in feeling and Christian courtesy in speech; to be slow to take offense, but always ready for reconciliation, and mindful of the rules of our Savior, to secure it without delay.

We moreover engage that when we remove from this place, we will, as soon as possible, unite with some other church where we can carry out the spirit of this covenant and the principles of God's Word.

Chapter 1

Salvation and Witnesses to the Covenant

Having been led, as we believe, by the Spirit of God to receive the Lord Jesus Christ as our Savior, and on profession of our faith, having been baptized in the name of the Father, and of the Son, and of the Holy Spirit, we do now in the presence of God, angels, and this assembly, most solemnly and joyfully enter into covenant with one another, as one body in Christ.

I. SALVATION

Salvation is a process that has three stages. The first stage is regeneration or the new birth. In regeneration, or the new birth, we are saved from the penalty of sin. The apostle Paul said, "For the wages of sin is death, but the free gift of God is eternal life in Christ Jesus our Lord" (Romans 6:23).

In regeneration, or the new birth, the mind is given a holy character. Paul said, "And do not be conformed to this world, but be transformed by the renewing of your mind, so that you may prove what the will of God is, that which is good and acceptable and perfect" (Romans 12:2).

Regeneration is effected by the power of the Holy Spirit. Jesus said to Nicodemus, "That which is born of the flesh is flesh, and that which is born of the Spirit is spirit. Do not be amazed that I said to you, 'You must be born again.' The wind blows where it wishes and you hear the sound of it, but do not know where it comes from and where it is going; so is everyone who is born of the Spirit" (John 3:6-8). Without regeneration there is no spiritual life. There is no human act that can substitute for this divine activity. Through regeneration, we are made partakers of the divine nature. The evidence of regeneration is seen in a godly lifestyle. There are two things necessary in regeneration—they are repentance toward God and faith in Jesus Christ. Repentance involves conviction, contrition, and conversion. After this conviction, contrition, and conversion, Jesus is trusted as Savior and followed as Lord.

The second stage in salvation is sanctification. The apostle Paul said the following to the Christians in Thessalonica:

> For this is the will of God, your sanctification; that is, that you abstain from sexual immorality; that each of you know how to possess his

own vessel in sanctification and honor, not in lustful passion, like the Gentiles who do not know God; and that no man transgress and defraud his brother in the matter because the Lord is the avenger in all these things, just as we also told you before and solemnly warned you. For God has not called us for the purpose of impurity, but in sanctification. So, he who rejects this is not rejecting man but the God who gives His Holy Spirit to you. (1 Thessalonians 4:3-8)

Paul said to the Corinthians, "But by His doing you are in Christ Jesus, who became to us wisdom from God, and righteousness and sanctification, and redemption" (1 Corinthians 1:30). *Sanctify* means "to hallow, to purify, or to consecrate." It suggests being set apart from a common use to a sacred use. It suggests devoting and dedicating a thing or person to the service and worship of God.

Sanctification does not mean a person has become sinless. The apostle John said, "If we say that we have no sin, we are deceiving ourselves and the truth is not in us. If we confess our sins, He is faithful and righteous to forgive us our sins and to cleanse us from all unrighteousness. If we say that we have not sinned, we make Him a liar and His word is not in us" (1 John 1:8-10).

The final stage in salvation is glorification. *Glorification* is the final state of righteousness which shall be fully realized in heaven. The apostle Paul said to the Romans, "The Spirit Himself testifies with our spirit that we are children of God, and if children, heirs also, heirs of God and fellow heirs with Christ, if indeed we suffer with Him so that we may also be glorified with Him. For I consider that the sufferings of this present time are not worthy to be compared with the glory that is to be revealed to us" (Romans 8:16-18).

The initiative in salvation is with God and not man. This is seen in predestination. Paul wrote about predestination in Ephesians 1:5. The word *predestined* (Greek: *proorizo*) means "to set boundaries or mark out beforehand." It means to determine before. This means that our salvation was secured in Jesus before the foundation of the world. God's love for us moved Him to predetermine our salvation. This predestination is the adoption as sons (and daughters). The word *adoption* (Greek: *huiothesia*) means "to place". It suggests giving sonship to a person to whom it does not naturally belong. This word was only used by the apostle Paul. He used it because he wrote primarily to Gentiles. Gentiles did not see themselves as having direct access to God and Jesus.

Jesus said, "No one can come to Me unless the Father who sent Me draws him; and I will raise him up on the last day" (John 6:44). This verse shows the initiative of God the Father in salvation. The word *draws* (Greek: *helkuo*) suggests being moved by power from within.

The apostle Paul also spoke of God's initiative in man's salvation. Paul said, "For it is God who is at work in you, both to will and to work for His good pleasure" (Philippians 2:13). The word *work* (Greek: *energeo*) means "to be operative; it means to display one's activity." The word *will* (Greek: *thelo* or *ethelo*) means "to have in mind." It means to be resolved or determined, to desire or wish. It means to take delight in a thing or person or to have pleasure. The word translated as "good pleasure" (Greek: *eudokia*) means "good will, kindly intent or delight." We were saved according to God's good pleasure. We were saved because our salvation satisfied God.

Salvation comes to any person who confesses Jesus as Savior. Paul said the following to the Romans:

> "THE WORD IS NEAR YOU, IN YOUR MOUTH AND IN YOUR HEART"—that is, the word of faith which we are preaching, that if you confess with your mouth Jesus as Lord, and believe in your heart that God raised Him from the dead, you will be saved; for with the heart a person believes, resulting in righteousness, and with the mouth he confesses, resulting in salvation. For the Scripture says, "WHOEVER BELIEVES IN HIM WILL NOT BE DISAPPOINTED." For there is no distinction between Jew and Greek; for the same Lord is Lord of all, abounding in riches for all who call upon Him; for "WHOEVER WILL CALL ON THE NAME OF THE LORD WILL BE SAVED." (Romans 10:8-13)

The word *confess* (Greek: *homologeo*) means "to agree with"; it means "to declare or admit." *Confess* means "to declare openly by way of speaking out freely." This confession is the effect of deep conviction. The word *confession* conveys the thought of declaring allegiance to Christ as Master and Lord.

After salvation, we were baptized as an outward sign of our relationship with Jesus. Baptism is a symbol of the death, burial, and resurrection of Jesus. It is the door into the local church. It is not essential to salvation, but it does symbolize our new life in Christ. Paul said, "Therefore we have been buried with Him through baptism into death, so that as Christ was raised from the dead through the glory of the Father, so we too might walk in newness of life" (Romans 6:4). The word *buried* (Greek: *sunthapto*) means "to bury together with." The baptism of a Christian declares that the person put faith in the expiatory death of Christ. His death gave us pardon from sins. Baptism symbolizes the fact that the former sinfulness is buried. It is completely taken away.

The Baptist church administers baptism according to the Great Commission. Jesus said in the Great Commission, "Go therefore and make disciples of all the nations, baptizing them in the name of the Father and the Son and the Holy Spirit" (Matthew 28:19).

II. WITNESSES OF THE COVENANT

We do now in the presence of God, angels, and this assembly, most solemnly and joyfully enter into covenant with one another, as one body in Christ.

In the church covenant, we commit ourselves to the principles of the Bible. If you will notice, the covenant is not made in isolation, nor is it made between God and man only. Church members are in a covenant with God and one another. Our covenant is made in the presence of God. God is omniscient and omnipresent. He is all-knowing and everywhere present. God is the Creator and Sustainer of the universe. He is sovereign in His will and infinite in His power. God is pure in His character and perfect in His conduct.

We should be aware that all our actions and attitudes are under the all-seeing eyes of God. Not only does God see and hear what we do and say, but also He is concerned about it. Therefore, we are accountable to God for our actions and attitudes. That makes the covenant a serious matter.

The covenant is also made in the presence of angels. Angels are messengers of God. They are a means by which God appears to mankind. They are a theophany. A *theophany* is an appearance of God. There were times when the appearance of angels was considered as the appearance of God Himself. God's appearance to Hagar speaks of this.

> Moreover, the angel of the LORD said to her, "I will greatly multiply your descendants so that they will be too many to count." The angel of the LORD said to her further, "Behold, you are with child, And you will bear a son; And you shall call his name Ishmael, Because the LORD has given heed to your affliction. He will be a wild donkey of a man, His hand will be against everyone, And everyone's hand will be against him; And he will live to the east of all his brothers."

Then she called the name of the LORD who spoke to her, "You are a God who sees"; for she said, "Have I even remained alive here after seeing Him?" (Genesis 16:10-13)

God's appearance to Moses is another example of an angel being a *theophany*, an appearance of God.

The angel of the LORD appeared to him in a blazing fire from the midst of a bush; and he looked, and behold, the bush was burning with fire, yet the bush was not consumed. So Moses said, "I must turn aside now and see this marvelous sight, why the bush is not burned up." When the LORD saw that he turned aside to look, God called to him from the midst of the bush and said, "Moses, Moses!" And he said, "Here I am." Then He said, "Do not come near here; remove your sandals from your feet, for the place on which you are standing is holy ground." He said also, "I am the God of your father, the God of Abraham, the God of Isaac, and the God of Jacob." Then Moses hid his face, for he was afraid to look at God. (Exodus 3:2-6)

The Lord appeared as angels because mankind cannot look at God and live. God said to Moses, "You cannot see My face, for no man can see Me and live!" (Exodus 33:20).

Although an angel is an appearance of God, the angel also has to be understood as distinct from God. This can be seen in David's punishment for numbering the children of Israel: "When the angel stretched out his hand toward Jerusalem to destroy it, the LORD relented from the calamity and said to the angel who destroyed the people, "It is enough! Now relax your hand!" And the angel of the LORD was by the threshing floor of Araunah the Jebusite" (2 Samuel 24:16).

The covenant is made in the presence of angels. Angels are messengers of God. The covenant is not only made in the presence of God and angels. It is made in the presence of "this assembly." The term *this assembly* has reference to the church where a person holds membership. When a person becomes a member of a church, that person becomes a vital part of each member of that church. This means that we have obligations and responsibilities to one another. A church can never be any stronger than the people who make up the congregation. This is why the covenant should be made solemnly and joyfully. It should be made in sincerity and joy.

A member of a church is a part of the complete body of Christ. Therefore, what we do or fail to do affects the whole body. The apostle

Paul wrote, "For just as we have many members in one body and all the members do not have the same function, so we, who are many, are one body in Christ, and individually members one of another" (Romans 12:4-5).

As members of the same church, we make up part of the body of Christ. The apostle Paul said it this way:

> For even as the body is one and yet has many members, and all the members of the body, though they are many, are one body, so also is Christ. For by one Spirit we were all baptized into one body, whether Jews or Greeks, whether slaves or free, and we were all made to drink of one Spirit. For the body is not one member, but many. If the foot says, "Because I am not a hand, I am not a part of the body," it is not for this reason any the less a part of the body. And if the ear says, "Because I am not an eye, I am not a part of the body," it is not for this reason any the less a part of the body. If the whole body were an eye, where would the hearing be? If the whole were hearing, where would the sense of smell be? But now God has placed the members, each one of them, in the body, just as He desired. And if they were all one member, where would the body be? But now there are many members, but one body. And the eye cannot say to the hand, "I have no need of you"; or again the head to the feet, "I have no need of you." On the contrary, it is much truer that the members of the body which seem to be weaker are necessary; and those members of the body which we deem less honorable, on these we bestow more abundant honor, and our less presentable members become much more presentable, whereas our more presentable members have no need of it. But God has so composed the body, giving more abundant honor to that member which lacked, so that there may be no division in the body, but that the members may have the same care for one another. (1 Corinthians 12:12-25)

Each member adds both strength and weakness to the body. When church members enter into covenant, we share mutual interests in the Lord's work. We also commit to maintain those mutual interests.

Chapter 2

Relationship to the Church

We engage, therefore, by the aid of the Holy Spirit, to walk together in Christian love; to strive for the advancement of this church, in knowledge, holiness, and comfort; to promote its prosperity and spirituality; to sustain its worship, ordinances, discipline, and doctrines; to contribute cheerfully and regularly to the support of the ministry, the expenses of the church, the relief of the poor, and the spread of the gospel through all nations.

Since we have been saved by God's initiative, and since the covenant we made is known by God, angels, and others, we pledge, by the help of the Holy Spirit, to live according to its teachings. The only way we can be what we should be is through the help of the Holy Spirit.

I. WALKING TOGETHER IN CHRISTIAN LOVE

We engage, therefore, by the aid of the Holy Spirit, to walk together in Christian love.

Walking together in Christian love is the way we show the nature of God. Here is what the apostle John said:

> Beloved, let us love one another, for love is from God; and everyone who loves is born of God and knows God. . . . Beloved, if God so loved us, we also ought to love one another. No one has seen God at any time; if we love one another, God abides in us, and His love is perfected in us. . . . We have come to know and have believed the love which God has for us. God is love, and the one who abides in love abides in God, and God abides in him. . . . If someone says, 'I love God,' and hates his brother, he is a liar; for the one who does not love his brother whom he has seen, cannot love God whom he has not seen. And this commandment we have from Him, that the one who loves God should love his brother also. (1 John 4:7, 11-12, 16, 20-21)

Not only does our walking together in Christian love show the nature of God, but also it is evidence of our being Christians. Jesus said, "A new commandment I give to you, that you love one another, even as I have loved you, that you also love one another. By this all men will know that you are My disciples, if you have love for one another" (John 13:34-35).

II. PROMOTING THE CHURCH WHERE YOU HOLD MEMBERSHIP

We engage, therefore, by the aid of the Holy Spirit . . . to strive for the advancement of this church.

The word *strive* means "to put forth strenuous effort." It means to labor hard or to work sincerely. As members of a church, that church deserves the best effort each member can give. We are a part of the church where we hold membership, and that church cannot be any better than the members make it.

As members of a church, you should not be constantly talking about how much better other churches are doing than yours. This is a reflection on you. If your church is nothing, that means the members are nothing. No man in his right mind will brag on another man's wife to his own wife.

The church where we hold membership should get no less than 100 percent of our talent, one-seventh of our time, one-tenth of our treasure, and 100 percent of our testimony. We should never use gifts outside our church we will not use in our church.

III. PROMOTING THE KNOWLEDGE OF THE CHURCH WHERE YOU HOLD MEMBERSHIP

We engage, therefore, by the aid of the Holy Spirit . . . to strive for the advancement of this church, in knowledge.

It is possible for a church to have more enthusiasm than knowledge. This is a dangerous state for a church to be in. The apostle Paul said to the Romans, "For I testify about them that they have a zeal for God, but not in accordance with knowledge" (Romans 10:2).

Enthusiasm without knowledge is like a fire out of control. Fire is good for heating and cooking, but fire out of control is destructive. It was misguided enthusiasm that caused Paul to persecute the church. Paul said of his actions, "Even though I was formerly a blasphemer and a persecutor and a violent aggressor. Yet I was shown mercy because I acted ignorantly in unbelief" (1 Timothy 1:13).

A church needs church members who are doing more than living virtuously. The church needs members who have knowledge of the

Word of God. The apostle Peter said, "Now for this very reason also, applying all diligence, in your faith supply moral excellence, and in your moral excellence, knowledge" (2 Peter 1:5).

Knowledge is a necessity to the effectiveness of Christian workers. Paul said, "Be diligent to present yourself approved to God as a workman who does not need to be ashamed, accurately handling the word of truth" (2 Timothy 2:15).

Knowledge is also dealt with in the Great Commission. Those whom the churches evangelize must be Christianized. Jesus said, "Go therefore and make disciples of all the nations, baptizing them in the name of the Father and the Son and the Holy Spirit, teaching them to observe all that I commanded you; and lo, I am with you always, even to the end of the age" (Matthew 28:19-20).

IV. PROMOTING THE HOLINESS OF THE CHURCH WHERE YOU HOLD MEMBERSHIP

We engage, therefore, by the aid of the Holy Spirit . . . to strive for the advancement of this church, in knowledge, holiness.

The word *holiness* (Greek: *hagiasmos*) means "sanctification." It suggests a separation to God. It means to be set apart for God's use. The apostle Paul said, "But by His doing you are in Christ Jesus, who became to us wisdom from God, and righteousness and sanctification, and redemption" (1 Corinthians 1:30). It also suggests the resultant state, the conduct befitting those separated to God. Paul said to the Christians at Thessalonica, "For this is the will of God, your sanctification; that is, that you abstain from sexual immorality; that each of you know how to possess his own vessel in sanctification and honor, . . . For God has not called us for the purpose of impurity, but in sanctification" (1 Thessalonians 4:3-4, 7). Sanctification is the state predetermined by God for believers, into which He calls them by His grace. When we accept the call to salvation we become saints.

As Christians, we are to bring holiness to its predestined end. In this way we will be found unblamable in holiness at the return of Christ. Paul said, "So that He may establish your hearts without blame in holiness before our God and Father at the coming of our Lord Jesus with all His saints" (1 Thessalonians 3:13). Holiness involves a right relation to God. Holiness is not an accomplishment. It is a state into which God in grace calls men.

As members of a church, we covenant ourselves to promote holiness in the church where we hold membership. Since we have been made holy, we should walk like we have been made. Paul said, "'Therefore, COME OUT FROM THEIR MIDST AND BE SEPARATE,' says the Lord. 'AND DO NOT TOUCH WHAT IS UNCLEAN; And I will welcome you. And I will be a father to you, And you shall be sons and daughters to Me,' Says the Lord Almighty" (2 Corinthians 6:17-18).

A church cannot have any greater holiness than the members' dedication to the Lord. Paul said to the Christians at Rome, "I am speaking in human terms because of the weakness of your flesh. For just as you presented your members as slaves to impurity and to lawlessness, resulting in further lawlessness, so now present your members as slaves to righteousness, resulting in sanctification" (Romans 6:19).

Holiness not only deals with what we should not be doing as Christians and church members, but it also involves what we should be doing and are not doing. If we are willing, God gives us the grace and the ability to fulfill His will for our lives. This is another dimension of holiness. Paul said to the Romans, "Therefore I urge you, brethren, by the mercies of God, to present your bodies a living and holy sacrifice, acceptable to God, which is your spiritual service of worship" (Romans 12:1).

God never asks more of us than we can give. Therefore, we are called upon to promote the holiness of the church where we hold membership.

V. PROMOTING THE COMFORT OF THE CHURCH WHERE YOU HOLD MEMBERSHIP

We engage, therefore, by the aid of the Holy Spirit . . . to strive for the advancement of this church, in knowledge, holiness, and comfort.

The word *comfort* means "to make strong." It suggests lessening the grief or misery of another by cheering or inspiring hope. *Comfort* suggests help and encouragement. It also suggests exhortation or advice. When we become members of a church, we owe comfort to the members of that church. Members of a church should never have to go through a rough time without the support of other church members. Paul said to the Thessalonians, "Therefore encourage one another and build up one another, just as you also are doing" (1 Thessalonians 5:11).

The New Testament word for "comfort" is a word (*paraklete*) which means "to call alongside." Jesus used this word in reference to the Holy Spirit in John 16:7; He said, "But I tell you the truth, it is to your advantage that I go away; for if I do not go away, the Helper will not come to you; but if I go, I will send Him to you."

If each church member is to promote the comfort of the church, each church member has to be led by the Holy Spirit. The Holy Spirit's using church members to comfort one another will create growth in the church. Luke said of the comfort of the Holy Spirit, "So the church throughout all Judea and Galilee and Samaria enjoyed peace, being built up; and going on in the fear of the Lord and in the comfort of the Holy Spirit, it continued to increase" (Acts 9:31).

Paul also said that there is comfort in the Word of God. Paul said to the Romans, "For whatever was written in earlier times was written for our instruction, that through perseverance and the encouragement of the Scriptures we might have hope" (Romans 15:4).

As members of this church, we covenant ourselves to strive, to put forth special effort to comfort, to encourage, to lessen the misery and grief of others.

VI. PROMOTING THE PROSPERITY AND SPIRITUALITY OF THE CHURCH WHERE YOU HOLD MEMBERSHIP

We engage, therefore, by the aid of the Holy Spirit . . . to strive for the advancement of this church, in knowledge, holiness, and comfort; to promote its prosperity and spirituality.

Promote (*promovere*) is a Latin word that means "to move forward; to further the growth of something." It means to work actively and stir up interest for the accomplishment of something.

Any person who is a member of a church has an obligation to make sacrifices for the good of their church. I use the word *their* because the church where we hold membership is ours by relationship, fellowship, and stewardship. The prosperity of a church will never be promoted if the members allow the church to operate on automatic.

Promoting the prosperity and spirituality of a church begins with the members sharing Jesus Christ with a lost world. Jesus said to His disciples, "But you will receive power when the Holy Spirit has come upon you; and you shall be My witnesses both in Jerusalem, and in all Judea and Samaria, and even to the remotest part of the earth" (Acts 1:8). When Jesus is shared, souls will be saved and the church will experience growth.

Church members can promote the prosperity of their church through their support of the work and the worship. The early church in Jerusalem is a clear example of what can happen when the members promote the work and the worship. Luke wrote about it:

> So then, those who had received his word were baptized; and that day there were added about three thousand souls. They were continually devoting themselves to the apostles' teaching and to fellowship, to the breaking of bread and to prayer. Everyone kept feeling a sense of awe; and many wonders and signs were taking place through the apostles. And all those who had believed were together and had all things in common; and they began selling their property and possessions and were sharing them with all, as anyone might have need. Day by day continuing with one mind in the temple, and breaking bread from house to house, they were taking their meals together with gladness and sincerity of heart, praising God and having favor with all the people. And the Lord was adding to their number day by day those who were being saved. (Acts 2:41-47)

In these verses, there are several things that characterize a church that promotes her prosperity and spirituality.

A. Love for Preaching (verse 41)

This church had a special love for preaching. They understood that the preaching of the Word of God was the means by which God would save all men who would believe. The time for preaching is the feeding time of the church. A church that feeds well on the Word of God promotes her prosperity and spirituality.

B. Receptive of Teaching (verse 42)

The word *doctrine* (*didache*) is active. The members of the church practiced the principles given them by the apostles. This church persisted in listening to the apostles as they taught. They followed the apostles' teachings without wavering.

C. Fellowship of the Saints (verses 42, 44-46)

The word *fellowship* reflects a growing sense of togetherness and of belonging. Those who were saved were received as additions to and members of the existing group.

In this church, all the members were together. They were bound into a fellowship by the same practices, the apostles' doctrine, and the breaking of bread. They were bound together by the same religious habits, prayer to God, and praise of God. They were also bound together by the same economic responsibilities. No one felt that anything he had was his own.

D. Regular Worship (verses 46-47)

The members of the early church never forgot to gather at the house of God. They applied the principles later written in the book of Hebrews: "And let us consider how to stimulate one another to love and good deeds, not forsaking our own assembling together, as is the habit of some, but encouraging one another; and all the more as you see the day drawing near" (Hebrews 10:24-25).

There was evidence of the early church's promoting her prosperity and spirituality in Acts 2:47. Luke wrote that they were "praising God and having favor with all the people. And the Lord was adding to their number day by day those who were being saved."

A church also promotes her prosperity and spirituality when she lives according to the fruit of the Spirit. Paul said to the Christians at Galatia, "But the fruit of the Spirit is love, joy, peace, patience, kindness, goodness, faithfulness, gentleness, self-control; against such things there is no law" (Galatians 5:22-23).

VII. SUSTAINING THE CHURCH'S WORSHIP, ORDINANCES, DISCIPLINE, AND DOCTRINE

We engage, therefore, by the aid of the Holy Spirit . . . to sustain its worship, ordinances, discipline, and doctrines.

A. The Worship of the Church

To *sustain* means "to support, maintain, to keep going as an action or process; to bear the weight of" a thing. Each member of a church should feel the burden of that church. Whenever worship is taking place, members should feel out of place when they are absent. To *worship* means to do honor or reverence to God. Worship is the time when we praise God and commune with Him.

In our worship, the activity results from what we believe. Worship expresses the inward realities of our spiritual lives. Worship is the dedication of the total person to God. It is the soul's movement into the presence of God. The word *worship* (*shachah*) means "to bend or bow." This does not necessarily speak of the body; it may also make reference to the soul. The bowing of the body and the soul helps our respect for God.

God is to be the object of our worship. Jesus said to the Samaritan woman, "But an hour is coming, and now is, when the true worshipers will worship the Father in spirit and truth; for such people the Father seeks to be His worshipers. God is spirit, and those who worship Him must worship in spirit and truth" (John 4:23-24). God seeks people who will worship Him in sincerity and honesty.

The worship of a church can only be sustained when the members are present and participate. Attendance at worship needs to become a habit. Each member of a church has an obligation to sustain the worship of the church where he or she holds membership. If the members do not sustain the worship, there is no one left to do it.

B. The Ordinances of the Church

The New Testament teaches that there are only two ordinances to be observed by the church. These ordinances are baptism and the Lord's Supper. These ordinances are object lessons.

Baptism symbolizes the death, burial, and resurrection of Jesus. Paul said to the Romans, "Therefore we have been buried with Him through baptism into death, so that as Christ was raised from the dead through the glory of the Father, so we too might walk in newness of life" (Romans 6:4). Paul said to the Galatians, "For all of you who were baptized into Christ have clothed yourselves with Christ" (Galatians 3:27). He said to the Colossians, "Having been buried with Him in baptism, in which you were also raised up with Him through faith in the working of God, who raised Him from the dead" (Colossians 2:12).

In baptism there must be a proper candidate, a saved person. There must also be a proper mode, which is immersion. There must also be the proper administrator. The proper administrator in the Baptist church is the Baptist preacher.

Immersion as the mode of baptism is seen in the baptism of Jesus. Matthew described the baptism of Jesus by saying, "After being baptized, Jesus came up immediately from the water; and behold, the heavens were opened, and he saw the Spirit of God descending as a dove and lighting on Him" (Matthew 3:16).

The encounter of Philip and the Ethiopian eunuch is another example of immersion being the mode of baptism. Luke wrote,

> Then Philip opened his mouth, and beginning from this Scripture he preached Jesus to him. As they went along the road they came to some water; and the eunuch said, "Look! Water! What prevents me from being baptized?" [And Philip said, "If you believe with all your heart, you may." And he answered and said, "I believe that Jesus Christ is the Son of God."] And he ordered the chariot to stop; and they both went down into the water, Philip as well as the eunuch, and he baptized him. And when they came up out of the water, the Spirit of the Lord snatched Philip away; and the eunuch no longer saw him, but went on his way rejoicing. (Acts 8:35-39)

The Lord's Supper symbolizes the suffering and death of Jesus. The Lord's Supper is a church ordinance. It should be taken only by persons who have been saved and baptized into the church. There are six things taught in the Lord's Supper.

It is a command. Paul said to the Corinthians, "Do this in remembrance of Me" (1 Corinthians 11:24b).

It is thanksgiving. "And when He had given thanks, He broke it, and said, 'This is My body, which is for you.'" (1 Corinthians 11:24a)

It is a memorial. Paul said, "In the same way He took the cup also after supper, saying, 'This cup is the new covenant in My blood; do this, as often as you drink it, in remembrance of Me'" (1 Corinthians 11:25).

It is a testimony for Christ. "For as often as you eat this bread and drink the cup, you proclaim the Lord's death." (1 Corinthians 11:26).

It is a confession of hope. "For as often as you eat this bread and drink the cup, you proclaim the Lord's death until He comes" (1 Corinthians 11:26).

It is also important to understand this: **The Lord's Supper is to be taken in the proper manner.** Paul said, "Therefore whoever eats the bread or drinks the cup of the Lord in an unworthy manner, shall be guilty of the body and the blood of the Lord" (1 Corinthians 11:27).

C. The Discipline of the Church

The discipline of a church has to do with causing church members to exercise obedience to the Word of God. A church that seeks to operate with church members' having the freedom to do whatever they want to do, whenever they want to do it, is a church of total confusion. Paul said to the Christians at Thessalonica, "We urge you, brethren, admonish the unruly, encourage the fainthearted, help the weak, be patient with everyone" (1 Thessalonians 5:14). The word *admonish* (Greek: *noutheteo*) means "to put in mind." It speaks of warning. It suggests cautioning or reproving gently. The word *unruly* (Greek: *ataktos*) is a military term that means "to be disorderly." It speaks of soldiers' not keeping rank. It means to be out of rank, out of one's place, undisciplined, or to behave disorderly. It means to break rank. This is a fitting term for Christians since we are in the Lord's army. And since we are in the army, we must follow the orders of Jesus, our Commander-in-chief.

Persons who walk in an unruly manner should not become a part of our company. Paul said, "Now we command you, brethren, in the name of our Lord Jesus Christ, that you keep away from every brother who leads an unruly life and not according to the tradition which you received from us" (2 Thessalonians 3:6). The word *aloof* (Greek: *stello*) means "to avoid." People who do not walk according to the discipline of the church should be avoided by those who do. Paul told the Thessalonians, "If anyone does not obey our instruction in this letter, take special note of that person and do not associate with him, so that he will be put to shame" (2 Thessalonians 3:14).

We sustain the discipline of the church when we encourage members in what is right and discourage them in what is wrong. We also sustain the discipline of the church when we stand firmly with the church and pastor when disciplinary actions are taken.

When we become members of a church, we pledge ourselves to walk according to the discipline of that church. Each church should be sure that what she requires of church members is based upon biblical principles.

D. The Doctrines of the Church

There are many people who seek to minimize the value of doctrine by saying it does not matter what you believe as long as you are sincere, but there are many people who are sincere but sincerely wrong. Doctrine is important to salvation and service. The word *doctrine* (Greek: *didaskalia*) suggests that which is taught. It means instruction or precepts. Doctrine also suggests a system or body of teachings related to a particular subject. Since we are Baptists, our doctrine relates to Baptists. This does not mean it is separate from the Bible. Baptist doctrine is Bible doctrine.

Paul said to Timothy, "All Scripture is inspired by God and profitable for teaching, for reproof, for correction, for training in righteousness; so that the man of God may be adequate, equipped for every good work" (2 Timothy 3:16-17). Our church should only be guided by the Bible. Jesus rebuked the scribes and Pharisees for teaching the doctrines of men. Jesus said of them, "You hypocrites, rightly did Isaiah prophesy of you: 'THIS PEOPLE HONORS ME WITH THEIR LIPS, BUT THEIR HEART IS FAR AWAY FROM ME. BUT IN VAIN DO THEY WORSHIP ME, TEACHING AS DOCTRINES THE PRECEPTS OF MEN'" (Matthew 15:7-9).

Church members sustain the doctrines of their church by learning them. Jesus said to the Jews, "My teaching is not Mine, but His who sent Me. If anyone is willing to do His will, he will know of the teaching, whether it is of God or whether I speak from Myself" (John 7:16-17).

We need to know the doctrines of our church because the knowledge of our doctrines prevents instability. Paul said this to the Ephesians:

> As a result, we are no longer to be children, tossed here and there by waves and carried about by every wind of doctrine, by the trickery of men, by craftiness in deceitful scheming; but speaking the truth in love, we are to grow up in all aspects into Him who is the head, even Christ, from whom the whole body, being fitted and held together by what every joint supplies, according to the proper working of each individual part, causes the growth of the body for the building up of itself in love. (Ephesians 4:14-16)

We sustain the doctrines of our church when we believe them. We do not practice what we do not believe. Or, we do not put much effort into what we practice when we do not believe it. That which we practice must come from the heart. Paul said the following to the Romans:

> "Do you not know that when you present yourselves to someone as slaves for obedience, you are slaves of the one whom you obey, either of sin resulting in death, or of obedience resulting in righteousness? But thanks be to God that though you were slaves of sin, you became obedient from the heart to that form of teaching to which you were committed, and having been freed from sin, you became slaves of righteousness." (Romans 6:16-18)

We also sustain the doctrines of our church when we teach them. We teach the doctrines of our church so that people might practice them. The early church was strong and effective because "they were continually devoting themselves to the apostles' teaching" (Acts 2:42).

Paul said to Titus, a young preacher of the Gospel, "Holding fast the faithful word which is in accordance with the teaching, so that he will be able both to exhort in sound doctrine and to refute those who contradict" (Titus 1:9). We are to hold to our doctrines so that we can encourage others and correct those who err. Paul also said to Titus, "But as for you, speak the things which are fitting for sound doctrine" (Titus 2:1). Sound doctrine is a necessary part of the speech of the Christian leader.

VIII. FINANCIAL SUPPORT OF THE PASTOR, CHURCH, MINISTRIES, AND MISSIONS

We engage . . . by the aid of the Holy Spirit . . . to contribute cheerfully and regularly to the support of the ministry, the expenses of the church, the relief of the poor, and the spread of the gospel through all nations.

God is not only concerned about the amount we give; He is also concerned about the attitude in which we give. Paul said concerning people who give liberally and purposefully, "Now this I say, he who sows sparingly shall also reap sparingly, and he who sows bountifully will also reap bountifully. Each one must do just as he has purposed in his heart, not grudgingly or under compulsion, for God loves a cheerful giver" (2 Corinthians 9:6-7). Our giving to God through our church should be liberal, purposeful, and cheerful. Verse 6 suggests that liberal giving increases our ability to give. In verse 7, the word *cheerful* literally means "hilarious." Our giving should not be because of any manmade laws, nor any feeling we may hold toward people in the church. Our giving should flow from a heart that loves God and His church. The kind of giving that pleases God is giving that comes out of the dedication of the giver. This is the kind of giving that should be done by each member of the church.

Each member of a church needs to know that he or she has equal responsibility for the financial support of the church. Every member should do as Paul wrote to the Corinthians concerning the missionary offering he was to receive for the poor saints in Jerusalem. Paul said to the Corinthians, "Now concerning the collection for the saints, as I directed the churches of Galatia, so do you also. On the first day of every week each one of you is to put aside and save, as he may prosper, so that no collections be made when I come" (1 Corinthians 16:1-2). In this passage, Paul called upon the Corinthians to do four things in their giving: he challenged them to give systematically, voluntarily, proportionately, and vitally.

When Paul considered the giving of the Christians at Macedonia, he used their giving as a motivation for the Corinthians. The Macedonians did not try to see how little they could give. Paul said of them the following: "For I testify that according to their ability, and beyond their ability, they gave of their own accord, begging us with much urging for the favor of participation in the support of the saints, and this, not as we had expected, but they first gave themselves to the Lord and to us by the will of God" (2 Corinthians 8:3-5). The Macedonians gave liberally because they gave themselves to Paul and the apostles before they gave their substance.

Paul also used the giving of Jesus to motivate the Corinthians:

> But just as you abound in everything, in faith and utterance and knowledge and in all earnestness and in the love we inspired in you, see that you abound in this gracious work also. I am not speaking this as a command, but as proving through the earnestness of others the sincerity of your love also. For you know the grace of our Lord Jesus Christ, that though He was rich, yet for your sake He became poor, so that you through His poverty might become rich. (2 Corinthians 8:7-9)

Giving has to be understood as a grace. It also has to be understood as a proof of our love. The motivating factor in our giving should be the example of Jesus. He was rich, yet he became poor so that we might become rich.

One area of giving that is most often minimized by both preachers and the laity is the financial support of the pastor. The Bible clearly teaches that it is as reasonable for a church to financially support the pastor as it is for a farmer to eat food from his garden, fruit from his fruit trees, or milk from his own goats or cows. Paul said, "Who at any time serves as a soldier at his own expense? Who plants a vineyard and does not eat the fruit of it? Or who tends a flock and does not use the milk of the flock?" (1 Corinthians 9:7).

When Jesus first sent His disciples out, He said to them, "Stay in that house, eating and drinking what they give you; for the laborer is worthy of his wages. Do not keep moving from house to house" (Luke 10:7). The reason why the disciples were not to carry anything with them was because those whom they were to serve were to be responsible for supplying all their needs.

Both the law and grace say a church should pay her preacher. Paul said the following:

> For it is written in the Law of Moses, "YOU SHALL NOT MUZZLE THE OX WHILE HE IS THRESHING." God is not concerned about oxen, is He? Or is He speaking altogether for our sake? Yes, for our sake it was written, because the plowman ought to plow in hope, and the thresher to thresh in hope of sharing the crops. If we sowed spiritual things in you, is it too much if we reap material things from you? If others share the right over you, do we not more? Nevertheless, we did not use this right, but we endure all things so that we will cause no hindrance to the gospel of Christ. (1 Corinthians 9:9-12)

Paul was quoting from Deuteronomy 25:4, as he wrote in verse 9.

The same principle by which the priests and Levites were supported by the children of Israel is the principle the church is to use in support of the pastor. Two passages of Scripture worth noting here are Numbers 18:21-28 and 1 Corinthians 9:13-14. Moses wrote these words:

> "To the sons of Levi, behold, I have given all the tithe in Israel for an inheritance, in return for their service which they perform, the service of the tent of meeting. The sons of Israel shall not come near the tent of meeting again, or they will bear sin and die. Only the Levites shall perform the service of the tent of meeting, and they shall bear their iniquity; it shall be a perpetual statute throughout your generations, and among the sons of Israel they shall have no inheritance. For the tithe of the sons of Israel, which

they offer as an offering to the LORD, I have given to the Levites for an inheritance; therefore I have said concerning them, 'They shall have no inheritance among the sons of Israel.'" Then the LORD spoke to Moses, saying, "Moreover, you shall speak to the Levites and say to them, 'When you take from the sons of Israel the tithe which I have given you from them for your inheritance, then you shall present an offering from it to the LORD, a tithe of the tithe. Your offering shall be reckoned to you as the grain from the threshing floor or the full produce from the wine vat. So you shall also present an offering to the LORD from your tithes, which you receive from the sons of Israel; and from it you shall give the LORD's offering to Aaron the priest.'" (Numbers 18:21-28)

Paul said, "Do you not know that those who perform sacred services eat the food of the temple, and those who attend regularly to the altar have their share with the altar? So also the Lord directed those who proclaim the gospel to get their living from the gospel" (1 Corinthians 9:13-14). Although methods might change from time to time, principles never change.

With many people, the church is "ours" when things are going well. When there are bills to be paid, then the church becomes "theirs." Every member of a church needs to know that a growing church has expenses. Each new member a congregation receives is an added expense to the church. The expense of that new member becomes the responsibility of the entire membership.

When 2 Corinthians 9:7 is considered, the principle of purposeful giving is suggested. Paul said in that verse, "Each one must do just as he has purposed in his heart, not grudgingly or under compulsion, for God loves a cheerful giver." God expects every person to support his or her church at the level of his or her ability. When each member carries his or her responsibility, no one will be burdened. Paul said the following to the Corinthians:

> For if the readiness is present, it is acceptable according to what a person has, not according to what he does not have. For this is not for the ease of others and for your affliction, but by way of equality—at this present time your abundance being a supply for their need, so that their abundance also may become a supply for your need, that there may be equality. (2 Corinthians 8:12-14)

People who really concern themselves with the expenses of the church are those who have first committed themselves to the Lord and the pastor. Here is what Paul said concerning the Macedonians: "For I testify that according to their ability, and beyond their ability, they gave of their own accord, begging us with much urging for the favor of participation in the support of the saints, and this, not as we had expected, but they first gave themselves to the Lord and to us by the will of God" (2 Corinthians 8:3-5).

It is also worth noting the issue raised in 1 Chronicles 29:5, 9. The writer said, "Of gold for the things of gold and of silver for the things of silver, that is, for all the work done by the craftsmen. Who then is willing to consecrate himself this day to the LORD? . . . Then the people rejoiced because they had offered so willingly, for they made their offering to the LORD with a whole heart, and King David also rejoiced greatly."

One reason our taxes are as high as they are is because churches fail to pay their tithes. Since the poor cannot be cared for through the ministries of our church, God uses our taxes paid to the government to support the poor. When it comes to the church meeting the needs of the poor, the first to be considered are the poor who are saints. Paul said to the Galatians, "So then, while we have opportunity, let us do good to all people, and especially to those who are of the household of the faith" (Galatians 6:10).

Each member of the church needs to know that he or she is responsible for the poor and the Gospel's being spread throughout the world. When you read 1 Corinthians 16 and 2 Corinthians 8–9, all of these are lessons on the church's response to the needs of the poor saints in Jerusalem.

The Gospel is the Good News of the saving work of Jesus Christ. It is God's power for salvation to all who believe it (see Romans 1:16). The apostle Paul would suggest that the spread of the Gospel is a good work. Here is what he said to the Philippians:

> I can do all things through Him who strengthens me. Nevertheless, you have done well to share with me in my affliction. You yourselves also know, Philippians, that at the first preaching of the gospel, after I left Macedonia, no church shared with me in the matter of giving and receiving but you alone; for even in Thessalonica you sent a gift more than once for my needs. Not that I seek the gift itself, but I seek for the profit which increases to your account. But I have received everything in full and have an abundance; I am amply

supplied, having received from Epaphroditus what you have sent, a fragrant aroma, an acceptable sacrifice, well-pleasing to God. And my God will supply all your needs according to His riches in glory in Christ Jesus. (Philippians 4:13-19)

The church that invests in the spread of the Gospel is the church that will have all her needs supplied by God.

The Great Commission is a message to the church that says the church's work is not limited to any race of people or any one place. The Gospel is for all people. It is universal in its scope. It does not seek to leave out anybody. It is always seeking the salvation of anybody and everybody.

Chapter 3

Relationship with the Family, the Community, and the World

We also engage to maintain family and secret devotions; to religiously educate our children; to seek the salvation of our kindred and acquaintances; to walk circumspectly in the world; to be just in our dealings, faithful in our engagements, and exemplary in our deportment; to avoid all tattling, backbiting, and excessive anger; to abstain from the sale of, and use of, intoxicating drinks as a beverage; and to be zealous in our efforts to advance the kingdom of our Savior.

I. MAINTAINING FAMILY AND SECRET DEVOTIONS

We also engage to maintain family and secret devotions.

The word *devotion* means "to sanctify." *To sanctify* means "to be set apart or separated." The one time the word *devotion* is used in the Scriptures, it refers to objects of worship. In Acts 17:23, Paul encountered people in Athens offering worship toward monuments built in honor of various gods. Among those monuments, there was one built in honor of the unknown God. Paul told the Athenians that it was that unknown God he wanted to tell them about. It is in the unknown God that we live, move, and have our existence. This makes Him worthy of our devotion.

Devotion is not limited to just one method. It may take the form of prayer, Bible reading, Bible study, witnessing, and even discussions on commitment to the Lord and His church. It should be understood that whatever habits we have at home, those habits we bring to the church. When the spiritual lives of families are low in the home, the spiritual life of the church will be low.

Each family member should have a special place in the home where he or she meets God on a daily basis. Jesus said, "But you, when you pray, go into your inner room, close your door and pray to your Father who is in secret, and your Father who sees what is done in secret will reward you" (Matthew 6:6).

Daniel's prayer life is a good example of having a special place to meet God. Daniel met God three times a day at the window in his bedroom that was opened toward Jerusalem (see Daniel 6:10).

The reason why family and secret devotions are so important is because they help in developing spiritual strength and Christ-like character.

II. RELIGIOUSLY EDUCATING THE CHILDREN

We also engage . . . to religiously educate our children.

To educate means "to develop, improve, teach, and train." Religious education takes place by precept and example. Children learn through what they read and hear; but they also learn through what they see. Each adult has an obligation to give children a good example to follow.

Religious education is important because through it children are brought to salvation. This is what Paul meant when he wrote to Timothy concerning his salvation. Paul said, "And that from childhood you have known the sacred writings which are able to give you the wisdom that leads to salvation through faith which is in Christ Jesus" (2 Timothy 3:15).

Religious education helps to keep children on the right course of life. Solomon said, "Train up a child in the way he should go, Even when he is old he will not depart from it" (Proverbs 22:6).

Parents may never give it, but we owe children religious education. We owe them religious education in the home and the church. There is some teaching that should take place in the home. There is also some teaching that should take place in the church. Parents should teach their children and lead them in learning and practicing the will of God for their lives while they are very young. Parents should also take advantage of what their church offers. Parents need what the children get from the church. With knowledge of the Bible backed by a strong conviction implanted in their souls by their parents, children will be much less likely to be problem children.

Religious education is designed to teach people how to live when others are not looking. The test of character is not what we do, say, or think when people are looking; but it is what we do, say, and think when we are alone.

Children who do not receive religious education must face the world without spiritual strength. These children live at a disadvantage. When there is no religious education, they will be left without some of the most important virtues they will need for living healthy lives.

While religious education should begin in the home at an early age, it should not be limited to home training. The church is a teaching agency. In the church, singing and religious music should be used to create a desire for sacred things in the lives of children.

III. SEEKING THE SALVATION OF FAMILY, FRIENDS, AND ACQUAINTANCES

We also engage . . . to seek the salvation of our kindred and acquaintances.

Whenever two people marry, both should be Christians. The Bible clearly teaches that Christians should not marry sinners. Paul said to the Corinthians, "Do not be bound together with unbelievers; for what partnership have righteousness and lawlessness, or what fellowship has light with darkness?" (2 Corinthians 6:14). However, if a Christian marries a sinner, the Christian should use his or her character and conduct in marriage to win the unsaved spouse. Marriages between the saved and the unsaved are according to God's permissive will, not His divine will.

Paul said that when a saved person marries an unsaved person the two should live together, with the saved person seeking the salvation of the unsaved person. Paul said the following:

> And a woman who has an unbelieving husband, and he consents to live with her, she must not send her husband away. For the unbelieving husband is sanctified through his wife, and the unbelieving wife is sanctified through her believing husband; for otherwise your children are unclean, but now they are holy. Yet if the unbelieving one leaves, let him leave; the brother or the sister is not under bondage in such cases, but God has called us to peace. For how do you know, O wife, whether you will save your husband? Or how do you know, O husband, whether you will save your wife?" (1 Corinthians 7:13-16)

Peter also wrote concerning Christians' wives and unsaved husbands, "In the same way, you wives, be submissive to your own husbands so that even if any of them are disobedient to the word, they may be won without a word by the behavior of their wives, as they observe your chaste and respectful behavior" (1 Peter 3:1-2). The saved spouse has an obligation to give his or her testimony, live a Christian life before the unsaved spouse, and not be a slave to worldly things. The greater a person lives a Christ-filled life, the fewer words that person will have to speak to his or her spouse. When people live like a Christian each day, others are more likely to hear their words.

Parents have a serious obligation to win their children to salvation. Parents' winning their children to Christ begins with the parents' living a Christian life before their children. Christian parents should also teach their children the Bible and to respect the church and the preacher. Paul said to fathers, "Do not provoke your children to anger, but bring them up in the discipline and instruction of the Lord" (Ephesians 6:4).

Solomon said, "Remember also your Creator in the days of your youth, before the evil days come and the years draw near when you will say, 'I have no delight in them'" (Ecclesiastes 12:1).

Not only do we have an obligation to seek the salvation of our families, but we also must seek the salvation of our friends and acquaintances. This is done by several methods. Paul said of himself that he used any means necessary to win others to Christ. Paul wrote,

> For though I am free from all men, I have made myself a slave to all, so that I may win more. To the Jews I became as a Jew, so that I might win Jews; to those who are under the Law, as under the Law though not being myself under the Law, so that I might win those who are under the Law; to those who are without law, as without law, though not being without the law of God but under the law of Christ, so that I might win those who are without law. To the weak I became weak, that I might win the weak; I have become all things to all men, so that I may by all means save some. (1 Corinthians 9:19-22)

One way we can win our friends and acquaintances is through inviting them to Sunday school and worship. We may also invite them to special events at our church, such as Vacation Bible School and revival. It has been said that friends should never let friends die without telling them about Jesus.

Christian members need to remember that we covenant ourselves to seek the salvation of our family, friends, and acquaintances.

IV. CHRISTIAN CHARACTER AND CONDUCT

We also engage . . . to walk circumspectly in the world.

Although every Christian has a private life, the life of the Christian is not totally private. Whatever a Christian does, or does not do, has an impact on other Christians. When we become members of a church, we covenant ourselves to walk circumspectly in the world. The word *circumspectly* (*akribos*) means "exactly, accurately, diligently, or carefully." Since we walk in the world, we must be careful that we do not become conformed to the world. Paul said to the church at Rome, "And do not be conformed to this world, but be transformed by the renewing of your mind, that you may prove what the will of God is, that which is good and acceptable and perfect" (Romans 12:2). Jesus prayed in His intercessory prayer, "I do not ask You to take them out of the world, but to keep them from the evil one. They are not of the world, even as I am not of the world" (John 17:15-16).

The world is so attractive that Christians have to be careful not to fall in love with it. John said in his first epistle, "Do not love the world nor the things in the world. If anyone loves the world, the love of the Father is not in him" (1 John 2:15). It was his love for the present world that caused Demas to desert Paul and go to Thessalonica (see 2 Timothy 4:10).

This portion of the church covenant challenges every church member to watch his or her step, since God and others are watching our steps. This means that Christians should avoid things that might cause the weak and the unsaved to stumble. Paul went as far as to teach the Corinthians that if the weak should even think that what the strong is doing is evil, the strong should not do it (see 1 Corinthians 8:1-13). He told the Thessalonians to avoid the very appearance of evil (see 1 Thessalonians 5:22).

As Christians, we should walk in the world as if we are walking in the presence of God. In fact, we *are* walking in the presence of God because there is no place where God is not. Our daily walk either strengthens or weakens our influence.

V. PERSONAL RELATIONS

We also engage . . . to be just in our dealings, faithful in our engagements, and exemplary in our deportment; to avoid all tattling, backbiting, and excessive anger; to abstain from the sale of, and use of, intoxicating drinks as a beverage; to be zealous in our efforts to advance the kingdom of our Savior.

There are several things involved in walking circumspectly in the world. Our walk in the world includes our personal relations. There are several things that should be a part of the life that walks accurately.

A. Honesty

We also engage . . . to be just in our dealings.

This means that Christians are to be honest and people of integrity. This honesty and integrity should cover every area of our lives. When we become Christians, dishonesty should immediately be put off. Paul said to the Ephesians, "Therefore, laying aside falsehood, SPEAK TRUTH, EACH ONE OF YOU WITH HIS NEIGHBOR, for we are members of one another" (Ephesians 4:25). A falsehood (Greek: *pseudos*) has reference to that which is said for the purpose of deceiving. Paul was concerned about these Christians' telling the truth because they were a part of one another. They could not lie to one another without lying to self and separating themselves. When we lie we dishonor one another and Jesus Christ. Those who live the new life in Christ are those who tell the truth.

When Christians lie, cheat, and commit injustices we give an untrue picture of God. Since we are to be like Christians in our character and conduct, we should be fair, honest, and upright in our dealings with others.

B. Faithfulness

We also engage . . . to be . . . faithful in our engagements.

Whenever a Christian makes an appointment, that person should keep it without hesitation. When a person does not keep an appointment, that person has lied. That which we do not plan to do, we should say we will not do it. One basis of our eternal reward will be our faithfulness. Jesus said, "His master said to him, 'Well done, good and faithful slave; you were faithful with a few things, I will put you in charge of many things; enter into the joy of your master'" (Matthew 25:21). The word *good* (Greek: *agathos*) speaks of being useful, upright, or honorable. The word *faithful* (Greek: *pistos*) speaks of persons who show themselves to be loyal or trustworthy in transacting business, executing commands, or discharging official duties. The faithful are those who are reliable. These are the ones Jesus will richly reward when He returns.

When we become members of a church, we pledge ourselves to support the life and work of that church. When the church where we hold membership is involved in her assigned tasks, those who are members should be present, or they are not faithful in their engagements. All of a church's work would be far more effective if the members of that church were faithful in their engagements.

C. Admirable in Conduct

We also engage . . . to be . . . exemplary in our deportment.

Christians are called upon to be examples in our conduct. This suggests clean and holy living in public and in private. In our living, our lives should be worthy of imitation for the sake of Christ. Paul once wrote to Titus, "In all things show yourself to be an example of good deeds, with purity in doctrine, dignified, sound in speech which is beyond reproach, so that the opponent will be put to shame, having nothing bad to say about us" (Titus 2:7-8). If our names are found painted on signposts, we should at least not supply the paint.

Paul also said to young Timothy, "Let no one look down on your youthfulness, but rather in speech, conduct, love, faith and purity, show yourself an example of those who believe" (1 Timothy 4:12). In both our words and our works, Christians are to be examples to the world. God expects us to live in such a way that others would want to be Christians because we are one. The work of salvation Jesus has wrought within us is to be demonstrated without. James said, "Even so faith, if it has no works, is dead, being by itself. But someone may well say, 'You have faith and I have works; show me your faith without the works, and I will show you my faith by my works'" (James 2:17-18).

People who are seeking to know the Savior want to see Jesus in our living rather than hear about Him from our lips. Since the church is to be made up of Christians, the world has a right to see Jesus in us. Jesus said the following:

> You are the salt of the earth; but if the salt has become tasteless, how can it be made salty again? It is no longer good for anything, except to be thrown out and trampled under foot by men. You are the light

of the world. A city set on a hill cannot be hidden; nor does anyone light a lamp and put it under a basket, but on the lampstand, and it gives light to all who are in the house. Let your light shine before men in such a way that they may see your good works, and glorify your Father who is in heaven. (Matthew 5:13-16)

Any person who is to be exemplary in conduct must live as Paul told the Philippians:

> Do all things without grumbling or disputing; so that you will prove yourselves to be blameless and innocent, children of God above reproach in the midst of a crooked and perverse generation, among whom you appear as lights in the world, holding fast the word of life, so that in the day of Christ I will have reason to glory because I did not run in vain nor toil in vain." (Philippians 2:14-16)

D. Avoiding Tattling

We also engage . . . to avoid all tattling.

The word *tattling* means "to blab, to inform on, to squeal, to gossip, to carry rumors, or to be a talebearer." These are things that hurt the reputations of other people. If we are to avoid all tattling, we must refuse to listen to gossip as well as refuse to participate in it. There is nothing positive about a tattler in the eyes of God. Solomon said concerning a tattler that "the words of a whisperer are like dainty morsels, And they go down into the innermost parts of the body" (Proverbs 18:8). This means that the words of a tattler are so tasty that people will gulp them down. Once they get down, they spread throughout the system. Solomon showed us here how quickly and how far a rumor can spread.

A tattler is another form of a slanderer. Solomon said concerning a slanderer that "he who goes about as a slanderer reveals secrets, Therefore do not associate with a gossip" (Proverbs 20:19). The tattler cannot be trusted. Solomon said that "he who goes about as a talebearer reveals secrets, But he who is trustworthy conceals a matter" (Proverbs 11:13).

When a person becomes a member of the church that person enters a covenant to avoid all tattling. I admit that this part of the covenant sometimes can be very hard to keep. One of the great causes of discord in the church is tattling. Church members need to work hard at bridling their tongues. This will help prevent the sowing of discord and will preserve peace in the church.

The tongue has set some fires that no one has been able to extinguish. James said, "So also the tongue is a small part of the body, and yet it boasts of great things. See how great a forest is set aflame by such a small fire! And the tongue is a fire, the very world of iniquity; the tongue is set among our members as that which defiles the entire body, and sets on fire the course of our life, and is set on fire by hell" (James 3:5-6).

E. Avoiding Backbiting

We also engage ... to avoid all ... backbiting.

When we become members of a church, we pledge that we will not backbite. *Backbiting* means "to attack another person's reputation and character behind his or her back." Backbiting is like a dog happily wagging its tail when facing you and then biting you when your back is turned.

A backbiter is a slanderer. It is a person who carries stories about other people from place to place and from person to person. The word *backbite* has for a root a word that means "to spy." It carries the idea of going from house to house getting information and passing it on.

Backbiting should be avoided because it disrupts church fellowship, shatters friendships, and weakens the influence of the church. If backbiting is to be avoided, we must not only stop doing it, but we must also stop listening to it.

Backbiting is so powerful that it adversely affects a person's worship. The psalmist wrote, "O LORD, who may abide in Your tent? Who may dwell on Your holy hill? He who walks with integrity, and works righteousness, And speaks truth in his heart. He does not slander with his tongue, Nor does evil to his neighbor, Nor takes up a reproach against his friend" (Psalm 15:1-3). Along with many others, the backbiter was listed by Paul as one who is worthy of death. Paul wrote,

> And just as they did not see fit to acknowledge God any longer, God gave them over to a depraved mind, to do those things which are not proper, being filled with all unrighteousness, wickedness, greed, evil; full of envy, murder, strife, deceit, malice; they are gossips, slanderers, haters of God, insolent, arrogant, boastful, inventors of evil, disobedient to parents, without understanding, untrustworthy, unloving, unmerciful; and, although they know the ordinance of

God, that those who practice such things are worthy of death, they not only do the same, but also give hearty approval to those who practice them. (Romans 1:28-32)

Backbiting could be avoided if Christians lived by the fruit of the Spirit. Paul said, "But the fruit of the Spirit is love, joy, peace, patience, kindness, goodness, faithfulness, gentleness, self-control; against such things there is no law" (Galatians 5:22-23).

F. Avoiding Excessive Anger

We also engage . . . to avoid all . . . excessive anger.

Excessive means to go beyond the usual or that which is necessary. It means to move beyond proper limits. Excessive anger is a powerful thing because it can hurt influence and wound so that a relationship is difficult to be healed. Paul would tell us that our anger should not lead to sin. He said "BE ANGRY, AND YET DO NOT SIN; do not let the sun go down on your anger" (Ephesians 4:26). Paul gave the reason for not letting anger simmer too long. He said, "And do not give the devil an opportunity" (Ephesians 4:27). When anger simmers, it goes deeper and deeper into the personality.

Excessive anger is most often displayed by a temper out of control. Solomon said, "A gentle answer turns away wrath, But a harsh word stirs up anger" (Proverbs 15:1). It is not so much what we say but how we say it that makes the difference in how our words are accepted. Solomon also said, "A hot-tempered man stirs up strife, But the slow to anger calms a dispute" (Proverbs 15:18). A temper out of control means that the tongue becomes a deadly weapon.

Any person who can control his or her temper should be commended. Solomon said, "He who is slow to anger is better than the mighty, And he who rules his spirit, than he who captures a city" (Proverbs 16:32).

Anger is a destructive force that will cause a person to forget God and God's work. It will cause a person to forget his or her own best interests. It will cause a person to forget the interests of his or her church and community. It should be avoided like avoiding a contagious disease. The best way to avoid excessive anger is to grow in tolerance of others. We must seek to maintain peace at any cost to us. Paul said, "Therefore I, the prisoner of the Lord, implore you to walk in a manner worthy of the calling with which you have been called, with all humility and gentleness, with patience, showing tolerance for one another in love, being diligent to preserve the unity of the Spirit in the bond of peace" (Ephesians 4:1-3).

When we become members of a church, we pledge ourselves to avoid excessive anger. We understand that excessive anger disrupts the fellowship of our church.

G. Abstinence from the Sale and Use of Intoxicating Drinks

We also engage . . . to abstain from the sale of, and use of, intoxicating drinks as a beverage.

This part of the covenant is probably argued more than any other. One reason for this is dependent upon the version of the covenant you are using. The version that contains these words was written during prohibition. There are some later versions of the church covenant that speak of the use of illicit drugs. Prohibition made the sale and use of intoxicating drinks as a beverage illegal. Since the prohibition of intoxicating drinks has been lifted, we must now decide on it strictly from a moral and biblical point of view. Let us consider some things the Bible says about the use of intoxicating drinks.

Solomon said, "Wine is a mocker, strong drink a brawler, And whoever is intoxicated by it is not wise" (Proverbs 20:1). The word *mocker* (Hebrew: *luwts*) means "to scorn, to make mouths at, to talk arrogantly." It means to boast, to be inflated. Intoxicating drinks give us false views of self and others. It makes people feel bigger than they really are. It is a great deceiver. When Solomon said that strong drink is a *brawler* (Hebrew: *hamah*), he was suggesting that it growls, roars, or rages. It puts a person in an uproar. Solomon would have us to know that any person who uses intoxicating drinks as a beverage is a fool.

Intoxicating drinks promise joy but they bring sorrow. Solomon said, "Who has woe? Who has sorrow? Who has contentions? Who has complaining? Who has wounds without cause? Who has redness of eyes? Those who linger long over wine, Those who go to taste mixed wine" (Proverbs 23:29-30).

Intoxicating drinks are powerful destroyers. They destroy reputations, character, lives, homes, job security, and nations. It was intoxicating drinks that brought shame to Noah. After the flood was over, he got drunk and lay naked inside his tent (see Genesis 9:21).

It was the use of intoxicating drinks that brought fornication into the home of Lot. The Bible reads:

> Now Abraham arose early in the morning and went to the place where he had stood before the LORD; and he looked down toward Sodom and Gomorrah, and toward all the land of the valley, and he saw, and behold, the smoke of the land ascended like the smoke of a furnace. Thus it came about, when God destroyed the cities of the valley, that God remembered Abraham, and sent Lot out of the midst of the overthrow, when He overthrew the cities in which Lot lived. Lot went up from Zoar, and stayed in the mountains, and his two daughters with him; for he was afraid to stay in Zoar; and he stayed in a cave, he and his two daughters. Then the firstborn said to the younger, "Our father is old, and there is not a man on earth to come in to us after the manner of the earth. Come, let us make our father drink wine, and let us lie with him, that we may preserve our family through our father." So they made their father drink wine that night, and the firstborn went in and lay with her father; and he did not know when she lay down or when she arose. On the following day, the firstborn said to the younger, "Behold, I lay last night with my father; let us make him drink wine tonight also; then you go in and lie with him, that we may preserve our family through our father." So they made their father drink wine that night also, and the younger arose and lay with him; and he did not know when she lay down or when she arose. Thus both the daughters of Lot were with child by their father. And the firstborn bore a son, and called his name Moab; he is the father of the Moabites to this day. And as for the younger, she also bore a son, and called his name Ben-ammi; he is the father of the sons of Ammon to this day." (Genesis 19:27-38)

Intoxicating drinks led to the death of Amnon. As it is recorded in the book of 2 Samuel, "Absalom commanded his servants, saying, 'See now, when Amnon's heart is merry with wine, and when I say to you, "Strike Amnon," then put him to death. Do not fear; have not I myself commanded you? Be courageous and be valiant'" (2 Samuel 13:28).

God warned Israel through Isaiah that intoxicating drinks bring misery. Isaiah said, "Woe to those who rise early in the morning that they may pursue strong drink, Who stay up late in the evening that wine may inflame them! . . . Woe to those who are heroes in drinking wine And valiant men in mixing strong drink" (Isaiah 5:11, 22). God wanted Israel to know that intoxicating drinks could lead to their ruin.

It was intoxicating drinks that led Belshazzar to call for the sacred vessels from the Temple in Jerusalem to be brought in to be used in his celebration in honor of a thousand of his nobles. His actions brought on his own death and the downfall of Babylon (see Daniel 5:1-31). God warned him of his death and the downfall of Babylon by writing a message on the wall of the banquet hall of the king's palace.

Intoxicating drinks affect sound judgment. This was said to Lemuel: "It is not for kings, O Lemuel, It is not for kings to drink wine, Or for rulers to desire strong drink, For they will drink and forget what is decreed, And pervert the rights of all the afflicted. Give strong drink to him who is perishing, And wine to him whose life is bitter. Let him drink and forget his poverty And remember his trouble no more" (Proverbs 31:4-7). The only persons who should drink intoxicating drinks are those who do not want to make anything worthwhile of themselves.

Because of intoxicating drinks, the prophets and priests in Isaiah's day made serious errors in doing God's will. They did not see what they should have seen, and they made bad judgments. Isaiah said, "And these also reel with wine and stagger from strong drink: The priest and the prophet reel with strong drink, They are confused by wine, they stagger from strong drink; They reel while having visions, They totter when rendering judgment" (Isaiah 28:7).

Intoxicating drinks are narcotics. They slow the mind and poison the body. They weaken character. Intoxicating drinks are so powerful that they are like the bite of a snake. Consider the following:

> Do not look on the wine when it is red, When it sparkles in the cup, When it goes down smoothly; At the last it bites like a serpent And stings like a viper. Your eyes will see strange things And your mind will utter perverse things. And you will be like one who lies down in the middle of the sea, Or like one who lies down on the top of a mast. "They struck me, but I did not become ill; They beat me, but I did not know it. When shall I awake? I will seek another drink." (Proverbs 23:31-35)

The apostle Paul told the Christians at Ephesus to not be overcome by intoxicating drinks. He said, "And do not get drunk with wine, for that is dissipation, but be filled with the Spirit" (Ephesians 5:18). The word *dissipation* speaks of a life of wastefulness. Paul was literally saying that the use of intoxicating drinks is not conducive for high and holy living.

When we become members of a church, we pledge to abstain from intoxicating drinks as a beverage.

H. Enthusiastic in Christian Service

We also engage . . . to be zealous in our efforts to advance the kingdom of our Savior.

The word *kingdom* (Greek: *basileia*) suggests kingly power or authority. It suggests the territory or people over whom a king rules. The kingdom of our Savior suggests the place where Christ rules. Despite all that is going on in the world, Christ has not surrendered His sovereignty.

He invites people to submit to His rule. Wherever Jesus is, His kingdom is there also. Jesus said that no one will say "'Look, here it is!' or, 'There it is!'" "For behold, the kingdom of God is in your midst" (Luke 17:21). Therefore, the kingdom of our Savior begins in the hearts of people. Then, Jesus is King in the church.

People enter into the kingdom of Christ by the new birth. Jesus said, "Truly, truly, I say to you, unless one is born of water and the Spirit he cannot enter into the kingdom of God" (John 3:5). There is nothing in human nature that can bring a person into the kingdom of God. There is but one kingdom, variously described: of the Son of Man (see Matthew 13:41); of Jesus (see Revelation 1:9); of Christ Jesus (see 2 Timothy 4:1); of Christ and God (see Ephesians 5:5); of our Lord, and of His Christ (see Revelation 11:15); of our God, and the authority of His Christ (see Revelation 12:10); of the Son of His love (see Colossians 1:13).

The Lord is looking for people who will be enthusiastic in their service for Him. We were not saved for us to sit idly by and wait for the return of Christ. Christ saved us to actively involve us in preparing people for His return. The apostle Paul said this to Titus:

> For the grace of God has appeared, bringing salvation to all men, instructing us to deny ungodliness and worldly desires and to live sensibly, righteously and godly in the present age, looking for the blessed hope and the appearing of the glory of our great God and Savior, Christ Jesus, who gave Himself for us to redeem us from every lawless deed, and to purify for Himself a people for His own possession, zealous for good deeds. These things speak and exhort and reprove with all authority. Let no one disregard you. (Titus 2:11-15)

The word *zealous* (Greek: *zelotes*) speaks of one burning with eagerness or enthusiasm. It means to be enthusiastic, energetic, or earnest. To be zealous suggests being most eagerly desirous of a thing. It means to defend and uphold a thing, intensely contending for a thing. This means that as a member of a church, I have a responsibility to put forth strenuous effort to move forward the kingdom of Christ from the church where I hold membership. This is one of the reasons for which the Lord saved us.

Enthusiasm for the service of Christ is contagious. This can be seen in what Paul said to the Corinthians as he was receiving an offering for the saints in Jerusalem. Paul said, "For it is superfluous for me to write to you about this ministry to the saints; for I know your readiness, of which I boast about you to the Macedonians, namely, that Achaia has been prepared since last year, and your zeal has stirred up most of them" (2 Corinthians 9:1-2). Most of the people who were giving offerings for the saints in Jerusalem were motivated by the Corinthians. Their enthusiasm had lit the fire of many others.

As important as enthusiasm is, misguided enthusiasm is dangerous. Paul's misguided enthusiasm caused him to persecute the church. He said concerning himself, "As to zeal, a persecutor of the church; as to the righteousness which is in the Law, found blameless" (Philippians 3:6). Paul's misguided enthusiasm caused him to persecute Christians when he should have been commending them.

It is misguided enthusiasm that leads away from salvation. Paul said this to the Romans:

> Brethren, my heart's desire and my prayer to God for them is for their salvation. For I testify about them that they have a zeal for God, but not in accordance with knowledge. For not knowing about God's righteousness and seeking to establish their own, they did not subject themselves to the righteousness of God. For Christ is the end of the law for righteousness to everyone who believes. (Romans 10:1-4)

It is sad to say, but there is often more enthusiasm where there is no knowledge than there is enthusiasm in the presence of knowledge.

When you focus on the church covenant, you will see that our enthusiasm should be for the progress of the kingdom of our Savior and not self. There are at least five things that will advance the kingdom of our Savior. They are (1) evangelism; (2) Christian education; (3) worship; (4) ministering; and (5) the stewardship of time, talent, treasure, and testimony.

Chapter 4

Living Together as Christians

We further engage to watch over one another in brotherly love; to remember one another in prayer; to aid one another in sickness and distress; to cultivate Christian sympathy in feeling and Christian courtesy in speech; to be slow to take offense, but always ready for reconciliation, and mindful of the rules of our Savior, to secure it without delay.

I. WATCHING OVER ONE ANOTHER IN LOVE

We further engage to watch over one another in brotherly love.

The word *watch* means "to keep awake and alert in order to look after." It means to protect or guard. It means to tend as a flock. As members of a church, we covenant ourselves to look after one another as a shepherd would tend a flock. The idea here is for us to look after those beyond just our friends and associates.

Love for one another is the greatest evidence that Christians have of being Christians. Jesus said to His disciples in His parting message, "A new commandment I give to you, that you love one another, even as I have loved you, that you also love one another. By this all men will know that you are My disciples, if you have love for one another" (John 13:34-35). The word *new* (Greek: *kainos*) suggests that which is unfamiliar, unused, unworn, unheard of, or uncommon. It suggests something that is new, not in time, but in form or quality. It speaks of being different in nature in contrast to that which is old. The word *commandment* (Greek: *entole*) means "an order, a command, a charge, a principle." It would be through the practicing of love that the world would know who the disciples of Jesus really are.

It is love for others that gives us the certainty of salvation. John said in his first epistle, "We know that we have passed out of death into life, because we love the brethren. He who does not love abides in death" (1 John 3:14).

The way Jesus told His disciples to practice love was not the usual and common way of practicing it. The way Jesus wanted His disciples to practice love was for His disciples to love others the way He had loved them. The usual and common way of practicing love is to love only those who love us in return. Jesus loved those who were even unlovely and unlovable. He sought the best good of all people.

Brotherly love is so powerful that it will prevent Christians from mistreating one another. Paul said to the Romans, "'YOU SHALL LOVE YOUR NEIGHBOR AS YOURSELF.' Love does no wrong to a neighbor; therefore love is the fulfillment of the law" (Romans 13:9b-10). Love keeps Christians from thinking and doing wrong toward one another. It positively controls our actions and our attitude.

It is love for one another that keeps Christians lifting other Christians above themselves. Paul said, "Be devoted to one another in brotherly love; give preference to one another in honor" (Romans 12:10). The word *devoted* (Greek: *philostorgos*) means "loving affection, prone to love or loving tenderly." It speaks chiefly of the reciprocal tenderness of parents and children. Paul was suggesting here that Christians should place more value on others than they do themselves.

Paul would have us to know that Christians do not reach a point where they do not need to improve in their love. He said to the Thessalonians, "Now as to the love of the brethren, you have no need for anyone to write to you, for you yourselves are taught by God to love one another; for indeed you do practice it toward all the brethren who are in all Macedonia. But we urge you, brethren, to excel still more" (1 Thessalonians 4:9-10).

II. REMEMBERING ONE ANOTHER IN PRAYER

We further engage ... to remember one another in prayer.

Prayer is the greatest and most unused power available to the church. This is probably true because we do not really understand what can be accomplished through prayer. Prayer is not just the sincere desire of the heart. It is entering the presence of God. When we do not pray, it is because we have resisted the movement of the Holy Spirit in our lives. Prayer is inviting Jesus into the events of life. It is giving Him permission to use His power to help us at the point of our needs. Prayer is an acknowledgment of our helplessness and the recognition of God's power to help.

Prayer is so valuable that Jesus taught His disciples to pray during His teachings in the Sermon on the Mount (see Matthew 6:5-13). It was something He practiced in His own life. It was the means by which He stayed in communication and communion with His Father. Jesus prayed often because His busy life demanded it.

If prayer is to be effective, then those who pray must have faith. Jesus said, "And all things you ask in prayer, believing, you shall receive" (Matthew 21:22). The word *believing* (Greek: *pisteuo*) means "to be persuaded of, to place confidence in or to trust." It means to rely on. If we expect God to answer prayer, we must believe He has answered, even before He has answered.

It is also important to understand that God answers prayer when we abide in Him and His Word abides in us. Jesus said, "If you abide in Me, and My words abide in you, ask whatever you wish, and it will be done for you" (John 15:7). Abiding in Jesus and His words' abiding in us gives us power with God. This is so because we conform to the will of God.

As we consider the power of prayer, we need to know that as members of a church we pledge ourselves to pray for one another. When church members fail to pray for one another, they hinder the growth and development of their church.

When church members remember one another in prayer, they cease to be selfish. They cease to pray the prayer of "me," "my," and "mine" only. When each person prays for others, everyone is prayed for. Remembering one another in prayer helps church members to love one another. We will not sincerely pray for people we do not love. James told his readers, "Therefore, confess your sins to one another, and pray for one another so that you may be healed. The effective prayer of a righteous man can accomplish much" (James 5:16). The word *effective* (Greek: *energeo*) means "to put forth power, to work effectually."

If we are to remember one another in prayer, we must first get to know one another. Prayer is most effective when it is specific. The only way we can pray specific prayers for one another is by getting to know one another. This involves interaction. This interaction is more than sitting on a pew with another person. It is actually relating to one another one-on-one. When this happens, we can effectively remember one another in prayer. This is a part of our responsibility as members of a church.

III. AIDING ONE ANOTHER IN SICKNESS AND DISTRESS

We further engage . . . to aid one another in sickness and distress.

This section of the church covenant shows how church members can demonstrate their love for one another. Love shows in works, and not in words. Times of sickness and distress are great opportunities to let people know we love them. Most church members expect the pastor to do all the visiting of the sick. They expect him to accept the responsibility to see that the needy are cared for. But when you consider the church covenant, you will see that as members of a church we pledge to visit the sick and help the needy. This expression of love is not just for those who are our closest friends or our relatives.

When we consider the sick and the needy, our first responsibility is to those who are of the household of faith. Paul said to the Galatians, "So then, while we have opportunity, let us do good to all people, and especially to those who are of the household of the faith" (Galatians 6:10).

John said concerning the needy and our relationship to them, "But whoever has the world's goods, and sees his brother in need and closes his heart against him, how does the love of God abide in him?" (1 John 3:17). The word *brother* (Greek: *adelphos*) has reference to a fellow believer, united to another by the bond of love. It speaks of brethren in Christ. The word *need* does not speak of whims and wishes. It speaks of the necessities of life. We have a spiritual obligation to meet the needs of people, and not their wishes.

Members of a church should approach each day with an open heart and open hands to help a brother or sister in need. When we minister to the needs of others, we minister to the needs of Jesus. This is what Jesus meant in Matthew 25:40-46. In that passage Jesus said this:

> "The King will answer and say to them, 'Truly I say to you, to the extent that you did it to one of these brothers of Mine, even the least of them, you did it to Me.' Then He will also say to those on His left, 'Depart from Me, accursed ones, into the eternal fire which has been prepared for the devil and his angels; for I was hungry, and you gave Me nothing to eat; I was thirsty, and you gave Me nothing to drink; I was a stranger, and you did not invite Me in; naked, and you did not clothe Me; sick, and in prison, and you did not visit Me.' Then they themselves also will answer, saying, 'Lord, when did we see You

hungry, or thirsty, or a stranger, or naked, or sick, or in prison, and did not take care of You?' Then He will answer them, saying, 'Truly I say to you, to the extent that you did not do it to one of the least of these, you did not do it to Me.' These will go away into eternal punishment, but the righteous into eternal life."

IV. CULTIVATING CHRISTIAN SYMPATHY IN FEELING AND COURTESY IN SPEECH

We further engage . . . to cultivate Christian sympathy in feeling and Christian courtesy in speech.

Love is not expressed through words as much as it is through deeds. John said in his first epistle, "Little children, let us not love with word or with tongue, but in deed and truth" (1 John 3:18).

When we become members of a church, each member should feel what is felt by others. When others hurt we should hurt also. When others experience joy we should experience joy. Christian sympathy in feeling can only be present in the absence of envy and malice. Paul said to the Christians at Rome, "Rejoice with those who rejoice, and weep with those who weep. Be of the same mind toward one another; do not be haughty in mind, but associate with the lowly. Do not be wise in your own estimation. Never pay back evil for evil to anyone. Respect what is right in the sight of all men" (Romans 12:15-17). We often like to step on people when they are down. But Paul suggested that we are to feel pain when others feel it and joy when others feel joy.

The reason we should feel what others feel is because we are members of one another. Paul said, "For just as we have many members in one body and all the members do not have the same function, so we, who are many, are one body in Christ, and individually members one of another" (Romans 12:4-5).

Christian sympathy in feeling will produce courtesy in speech. A kind word is the most inexpensive thing that church members can give one another. Any person who can control his or her tongue can control other actions. James said, "For we all stumble in many ways. If anyone does not stumble in what he says, he is a perfect man, able to bridle the whole body as well" (James 3:2).

Most of the time, we only think about what we say. But we also need to consider how we say what we say. The right thing said in the wrong way can lessen the effect of what was said. Solomon said, "A man has joy in an apt answer, And how delightful is a timely word!" (Proverbs 15:23).

Solomon also said, "Like apples of gold in settings of silver Is a word spoken in right circumstances" (Proverbs 25:11). Saying the right thing in the right way may not come naturally, but we can at least work at it to cultivate it.

Christian sympathy in feeling and courtesy in speech are two things we owe one another as members of this church.

V. MAINTAINING RELATIONSHIPS

We further engage . . . to be slow to take offense, but always ready for reconciliation, and mindful of the rules of our Savior, to secure it without delay.

As we focus on this section of the covenant, the emphasis is not on the person who does the offending—it is on the person who is offended. This section suggests that Christians should not wear their feelings on their shoulders. We must learn to tolerate the faults and failures of others, even those who may not be pleasing and pleasant toward us.

Paul said to the Ephesians, "Therefore I, the prisoner of the Lord, implore you to walk in a manner worthy of the calling with which you have been called, with all humility and gentleness, with patience, showing tolerance for one another in love, being diligent to preserve the unity of the Spirit in the bond of peace" (Ephesians 4:1-3). If you will notice this passage, there are four things necessary in walking in a manner worthy of the calling with which we have been called. They are (1) humility, (2) gentleness, (3) patience, and (4) forbearance of one another in love. These things are necessary if we are going to maintain unity. Paul suggested here that unity is something that requires strenuous effort to maintain. It does not come automatically.

Paul also discussed the issue of maintaining relationships with the Colossians. He said, "So, as those who have been chosen of God, holy and beloved, put on a heart of compassion, kindness, humility, gentleness and patience; bearing with one another, and forgiving each other, whoever has a complaint against anyone; just as the Lord forgave you, so also should you. Beyond all these things put on love, which is the perfect bond of unity" (Colossians 3:12-14). If relationships are to be maintained, people must learn to accept others as they are. Bearing with one another is not trying to change people into what we want them to be. It is accepting them without complaint. People need to be given the chance to be who they are.

One reason why relationships are not maintained is because people speak more than they listen. The mouth opens more quickly than the ears. James said, "But everyone must be quick to hear, slow to speak and slow to anger; for the anger of man does not achieve the righteousness of God" (James 1:19-20).

Solomon said this concerning those who do not easily become angry: "He who is slow to anger has great understanding, But he who is quick-tempered exalts folly" (Proverbs 14:29).

When love controls our lives, we will develop patience with others. Paul said that "love is patient, love is kind and is not jealous; love does not brag and is not arrogant" (1 Corinthians 13:4).

Whenever there is a broken relationship among Christians, that relationship should be mended immediately. Reconciliation is at the heart of Christianity. It is the ministry given to us by Jesus Christ. Paul said to the Corinthians, "Now all these things are from God, who reconciled us to Himself through Christ and gave us the ministry of reconciliation, namely, that God was in Christ reconciling the world to Himself, not counting their trespasses against them, and He has committed to us the word of reconciliation" (2 Corinthians 5:18-19).

Whenever there are broken relationships, Christians should practice the mission given to us by Jesus. It is bad for our testimony when we proclaim one thing and practice another. The life of the Christian should be guided by the Word of God. The Word of God teaches that when anger occurs, it should not linger. Paul said to the Christians at Ephesus, "Therefore, laying aside falsehood, SPEAK TRUTH EACH ONE OF YOU WITH HIS NEIGHBOR, for we are members of one another. BE ANGRY, AND YET DO NOT SIN; do not let the sun go down on your anger, and do not give the devil an opportunity" (Ephesians 4:25-27).

Broken relationships are detrimental to effective and meaningful worship. Jesus said in the Sermon on the Mount, "Therefore if you are presenting your offering at the altar, and there remember that your brother has something against you, leave your offering there before the altar, and go your way; first be reconciled to your brother, and then come and present your offering" (Matthew 5:23-24).

Chapter 5

Church Membership

We moreover engage that when we remove from this place we will, as soon as possible, unite with some other church where we can carry out the spirit of this covenant and the principles of God's Word.

Any person who is saved should want to be an active member of a local church. This means that wherever we live we should hold membership at a church there. Moving one's church membership should not occur after many years of drifting from church to church. Church membership should be moved as soon as possible after moving to a new city.

There are two ways in which a person can move his or her church membership from one Baptist church to another. One is by letter, and the other is by Christian experience.

Joining a church by letter means that a person goes from one Baptist church to another Baptist church with a letter of recommendation. The idea of a letter of recommendation is seen in Acts 18:27. Although this was not the moving of church membership, the idea of recommendation is advocated. In this passage, the Christians in Ephesus recommended Apollos to the churches in Achaia. The passage reads, "And when he wanted to go across to Achaia, the brethren encouraged him and wrote to the disciples to welcome him; and when he had arrived, he helped greatly those who had believed through grace; for he powerfully refuted the Jews in public, demonstrating by the Scriptures that Jesus was the Christ" (Acts 18:27-28).

The letter of recommendation helps a church to know something about the character and conduct of the person coming into the fellowship. There was a time in the life of the apostle Paul when the Corinthians treated him so rudely that he asked them if he needed a letter of recommendation for them to accept him. He said, "Are we beginning to commend ourselves again? Or do we need, as some, letters of commendation to you or from you? You are our letter, written in our hearts, known and read by all men; being manifested that you are a letter of Christ, cared for by us, written not with ink, but with the Spirit of the living God, not on tablets of stone, but on tablets of human hearts" (2 Corinthians 3:1-3).

The other way a person can move his or her church membership from one Baptist church to another is by Christian experience. Christian experience suggests that a person is saved but he or she is not eligible for a letter of recommendation from his or her church. That person may not be able to get a letter because he or she has been out of church for such a long period of time that the church could not recommend him or her.

Another reason why a person would join a church by Christian experience is because the church where he or she held membership has disbanded. The only thing left is for that prospective church to accept his or her statement of salvation.

A person should move his or her church membership after moving to a new city so that he or she can carry out the spirit of the covenant. It is very difficult to carry out the principles of this covenant when we cannot attend the church where we hold membership. The church where we hold membership is the place where we are to practice our discipleship.

We owe Christ and His church our deepest loyalty. Our loyalty to our church is an evidence of our level of love for Christ and His church.

Although the church covenant is not the inspired Word of God, it does contain some very important biblical principles worthy of practicing in our daily lives, our communities, our families, and our churches. Church membership carries with it privileges and obligations. As we enjoy the privileges, we should assume the obligations. Many of those obligations are taught in this covenant.

About the Author

THE REVEREND GEORGE T. BROOKS SR. received a bachelor of arts degree from the American Baptist College, where he was an outstanding honor student; a Master of Divinity degree from Faith Evangelical Seminary in Tacoma, Washington; and a Doctor of Divinity degree from the Shiloh Theological Seminary in Stafford, Virginia.

He is married to Sarah Brooks and has a daughter, Octavia; a son, the Rev. George T. Brooks Jr.; and five grandchildren.

The Rev. Brooks, who once pastored Friendship Baptist Church in Cross Plains, Tennessee, is presently pastor of Saint James Missionary Baptist Church in Nashville, Tennessee, where he has served since June of 1984. By the leading of the Holy Spirit, his consistent challenge to the church is to strive to become "A Church to Match This Hour."

He has been very active in religious and civic activities. He served as Director of Pastoral Studies Field Work and Practical Christian Service at American Baptist College for three years. He is a former commissioner of the Historical Commission and the Human Relation Commissions of Metropolitan Nashville-Davidson County. He is a member of 100 Black Men of Middle Tennessee. He served two years as Second Vice Moderator of the Little Fork District Association, seven years as President of the Congress of the Missionary Baptist State Convention of Tennessee, two years as Deputy Secretary of the Christian Education Board of the National Baptist Convention of America, Inc., and two years as the Chairman of that same board. He served as the Second Vice Moderator of the Nashville City Missionary Baptist District Association for eight years.

In October of 1995, he was elected president of the Missionary Baptist State Convention of Tennessee, which gave him leadership to some 130 churches in the Middle Tennessee area. He served until July of 2003. He was appointed Director of the Congress of Christian Workers of the National Baptist Convention of America, Inc. in September of 2003 and served until September of 2009. He was then appointed Fourth Vice President.

Out of his concern for the community, he and the church gave two lots to Habitat for Humanity, housing non-church members. This venture created an interest at heart that led him to a joint venture between the church and the private sector to develop and build fifty-two affordable houses.

He has received numerous awards and has written eleven books, including *Fruits of Fellowship*; *Believing as Baptists*; *Praising and Worshiping God*; *The Pastor's Love Offering*; *Saved, Satisfied and Secure*; *Offering God My Substance and Myself*; *Great Sermons from Our Past*; *The Letter to the Colossians*; *From the Heart of the President*; and *God's Use of a Man Called Nehemiah*. Many of his books are now available on WORDsearch®, one of the most comprehensive computer Bible programs available today.

www.ingramcontent.com/pod-product-compliance
Lightning Source LLC
Chambersburg PA
CBHW071545080526
44588CB00011B/1800